# First
# Dictionary

## Dear reader

Use this dictionary to help you with your reading and writing. There are pictures to help you read each word and a puzzle on every page for you to solve.

# Aa

airport

ambulance

ant

apple

apron

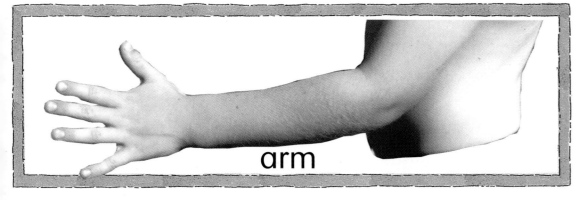
arm

**Find the insect.**

a b c d e f g h i j k l m n o p q r s t u v w x y z

# Bb

baby

bag

ball

balloon

banana

basket

**Find the toy.**

4

# B b

bath

beach

beans

bed

bee

bicycle

**What can you eat?**

a
b
c
d
e
f
g
h
i
j
k
l
m
n
o
p
q
r
s
t
u
v
w
x
y
z

5

a
b
c
d
e
f
g
h
i
j
k
l
m
n
o
p
q
r
s
t
u
v
w
x
y
z

# Bb

bird

black

blue

boat

book

boy

**What can fly?**

# Bb

bread

bridge

brown

butter

butterfly

button

*What is made from milk?*

a b c d e f g h i j k l m n o p q r s t u v w x y z

# Cc

calf

camel

castle

cat

caterpillar

chair

clown

*Find the baby cow.*

# Cc

computer

cow

crab

crayons

crocodile

cup

**Find the shellfish.**

a
b
**C**
d
e
f
g
h
i
j
k
l
m
n
o
p
q
r
s
t
u
v
w
x
y
z

# Dd

desk

dice

dinosaur

dog

doll

dolphin

*What lives in the sea?*

# Dd

donkey

door

dragon

dress

drum

duck

*What do you open?*

a b c **d** e f g h i j k l m n o p q r s t u v w x y z

11

# Ee

a b c d e f g h i j k l m n o p q r s t u v w x y z

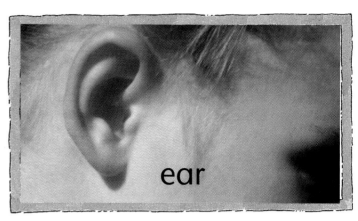
ear

egg

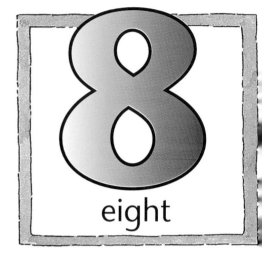
eight

elephant

envelope

eyes

**What do you see with?**

# Ff

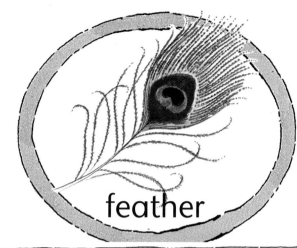
feather

fire

fish

five

flowers

fly

foal

**Find the baby horse.**

a b c d e f g h i j k l m n o p q r s t u v w x y z

13

# Ff

forest

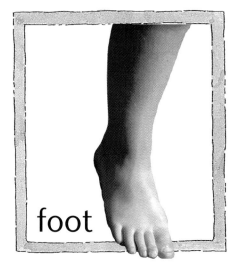
foot

fork

four

fox

frog

fruit

a b c d e f g h i j k l m n o p q r s t u v w x y z

**What do we use to eat with?**

# Gg

garden

gate

ghost

girl

glass

globe

*What can you drink from?*

# Gg

glove

gorilla

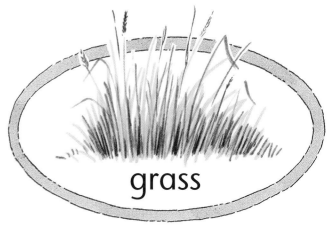
grass

grasshopper

green

guitar

**What can hop?**

# Hh

half

hamburger

hammer

hand

hat

head

**What do you hit a nail with?**

a b c d e f g **h** i j k l m n o p q r s t u v w x y z

17

# Hh

a b c d e f g **h** i j k l m n o p q r s t u v w x y z

helicopter

hen

hippopotamus

hole

horse

house

**What do people live in?**

18

# Ii

icicle

ice cream

insects

iron

island

**What do you eat on a hot day?**

a
b
c
d
e
f
g
h
i
j
k
l
m
n
o
p
q
r
s
t
u
v
w
x
y
z

19

# Jj

jacket

jam

jeans

jeep

jigsaw

jug

**What can you pour milk from?**

# Kk

kangaroo

kettle

key

king

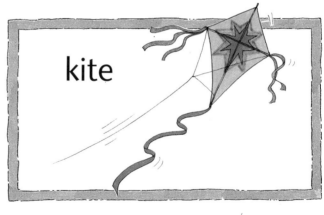
kite

kitten

koala

a b c d e f g h i j **k** l m n o p q r s t u v w x y z

**What do you fly in the sky?**

# Ll

ladder

lamp

leaf

lemon

lion

lizard

**Find the animal that roars.**

# Mm

magnet

man

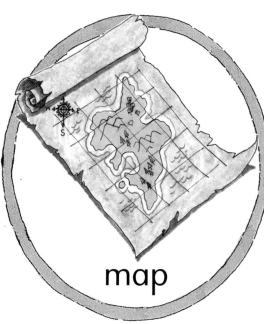
map

mask

microwave

milk

a b c d e f g h i j k l **m** n o p q r s t u v w x y z

*What do you use to find your way?*

# Mm

a b c d e f g h i j k l **m** n o p q r s t u v w x y z

mirror

monkey

monster

Moon

mountain

mouse

mushrooms

*What can you see your face in?*

24

# Nn

nail

necklace

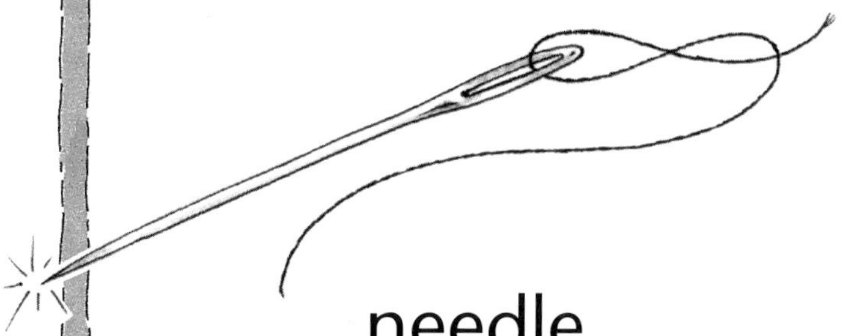

needle

nest

9
nine

nurse

nuts

*What do birds live in?*

# Oo

a b c d e f g h i j k l m n O p q r s t u v w x y z

octopus

1
one

onion

orange

ostrich

owl

**What has eight legs?**

# Pp

paint

paper

parachute

pear

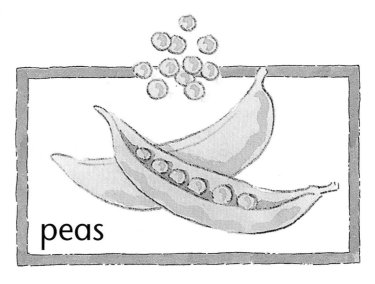
peas

**Find the fruit.**

a b c d e f g h i j k l m n o **p** q r s t u v w x y z

27

# Pp

a b c d e f g h i j k l m n o p q r s t u v w x y z

pencil

penguin

piano

picture

pie

pillow

**Find the object that you can write with.**

# P p

pineapple

pink

plant

puppet

puppy

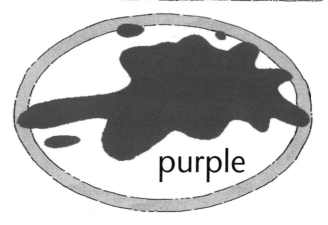
purple

*Find the baby dog.*

a
b
c
d
e
f
g
h
i
j
k
l
m
n
o
p
q
r
s
t
u
v
w
x
y
z

# Qq

a b c d e f g h i j k l m n o p **q** r s t u v w x y z

quarter

queen

question mark

quilt

*Find the King's wife.*

30

# Rr

rabbit

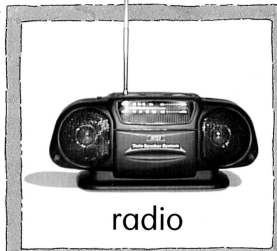

radio

rain

rainbow

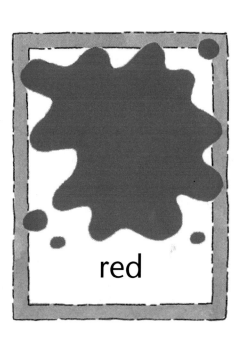

red

*What lives in a burrow?*

a b c d e f g h i j k l m n o p q **r** s t u v w x y z

# Rr

a b c d e f g h i j k l m n o p q **r** s t u v w x y z

ring

river

robot

rocket

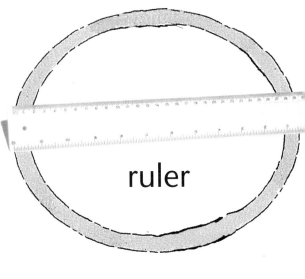

ruler

**What would you wear on a finger?**

# Ss

sandwich

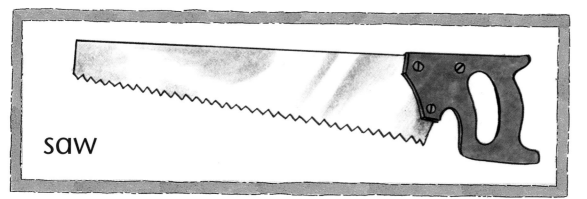
saw

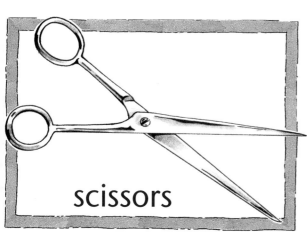
scissors

seven

six

skeleton

**Find the tool.**

# Ss

snail

snake

snowman

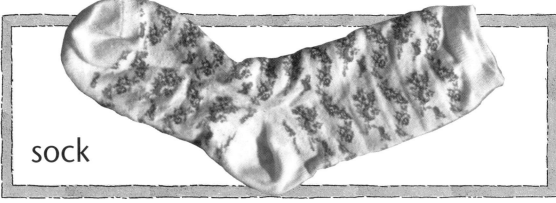

sock

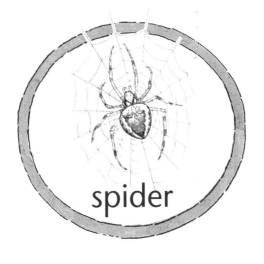

spider

spoon

*What do you put on your foot?*

# Ss

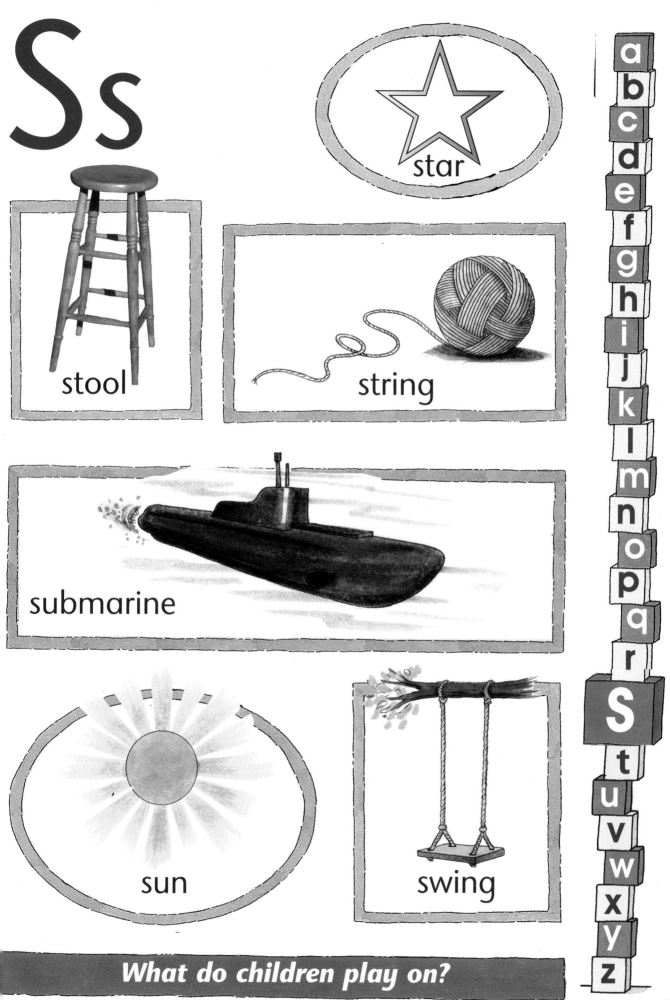

star

stool

string

submarine

sun

swing

**What do children play on?**

a b c d e f g h i j k l m n o p q r **S** t u v w x y z

# Tt

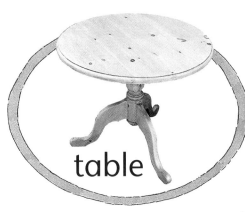
table

tadpole

tail

teddy bear

telephone

television

ten

*Find part of a dog.*

# Tt

three

tiger

tomato

toothbrush

towel

a b c d e f g h i j k l m n o p q r s **t** u v w x y z

**Find the fruit.**

# Tt

tractor

toys

train

tree

trumpet

turtle

two

*What does a farmer use on the farm?*

# Uu

umbrella

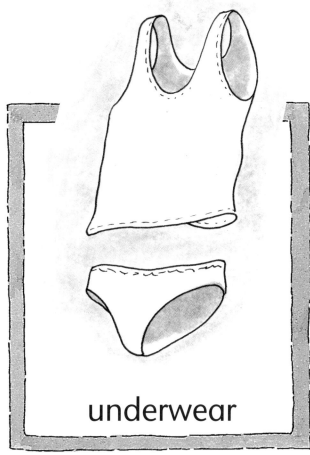

underwear

unicorn

uniform

*What keeps you from getting wet?*

# Vv

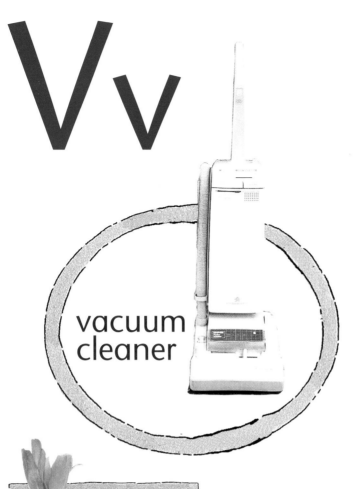

vacuum cleaner

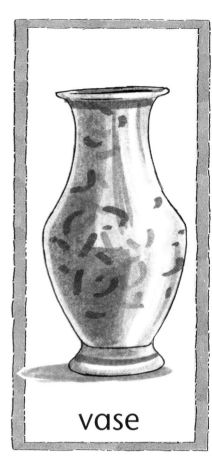

vase

vegetables

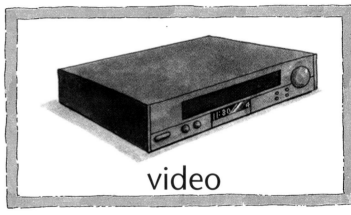

video

violin

volcano

**What would you put flowers in?**

# Ww

watch

water

waterfall

whale

wheel

wheelbarrow

a b c d e f g h i j k l m n o p q r s t u v **W** x y z

**What would you use in the garden?**

# Ww

**a b c d e f g h i j k l m n o p q r s t u v W x y z**

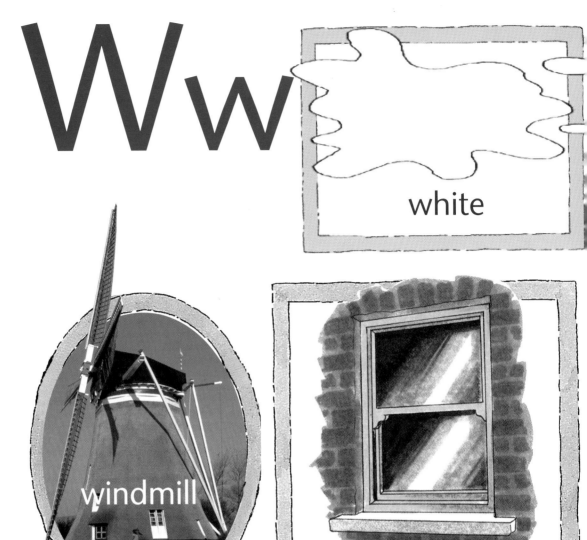

white

windmill

window

woman

wood

*What is made of glass?*

# X x

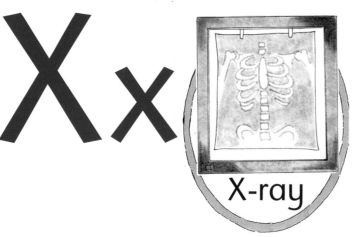
X-ray

xylophone

# Y y

yacht

yawn

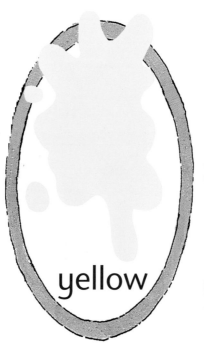
yellow

yo-yo

**What can you play a tune on?**

a
b
c
d
e
f
g
h
i
j
k
l
m
n
o
p
q
r
s
t
u
v
w
X
y
z

43

a b c d e f g h i j k l m n o p q r s t u v w x y z

# Zz

zebra

zero

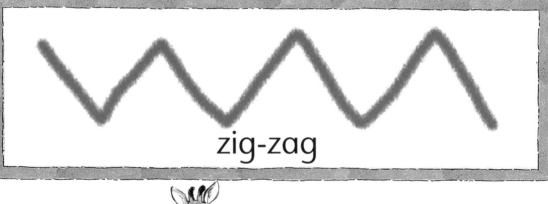

zig-zag

zoo

**Find the animal with stripes.**

# Words we often use

**Aa**
a
about
after
again
all
am
and
are
as
at
away

**Bb**
back
be
big
but

**Cc**
came
can
come
coming
could

**Dd**
day
did
do
does
doing
down

**Ee**
every
everyone

**Ff**
fell
for
from

**Gg**
get
getting
go
going
good
got

**Hh**
had
has
have
having
he
her
here
him
his
how

**Ii**
I
if
in
into
is
it

**Ll**
like
little
look
looking

**Mm**
made
me
more
my

**Nn**
name
new
no
not
now

**Oo**
of
off
old
on
once
or
other
our
out
outside
over

**Pp**
play
played
playing
put
putting

**Ss**
said
saw
says
see
she
so
some

**Tt**
that
the
their
them
then
there
these
they
this
to
too

**Uu**
under
up
upon
us

**Vv**
very

**Ww**
want
was
we
went
were
what
when
where
which
who
will
with

**Yy**
yes
you
your

a
b
c
d
e
f
g
h
i
j
k
l
m
n
o
p
q
r
s
t
u
v
w
x
y
z

# Numbers

**1**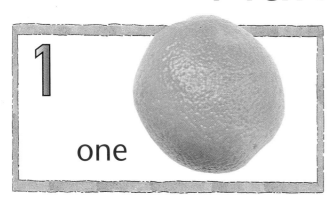
one

**2**
two

**3**
three

**4**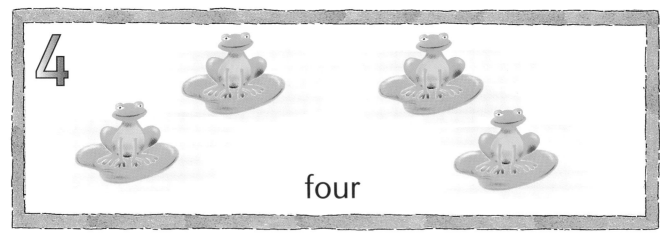
four

**5**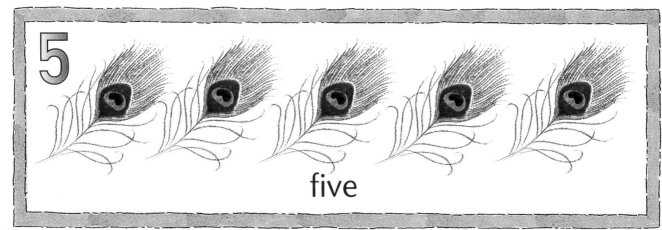
five

# Numbers

6 six

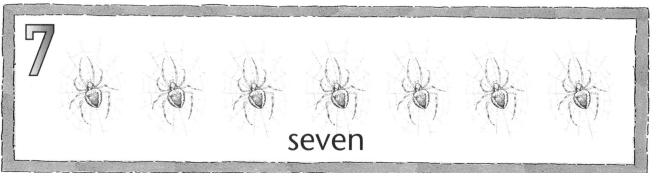
7 seven

8 eight

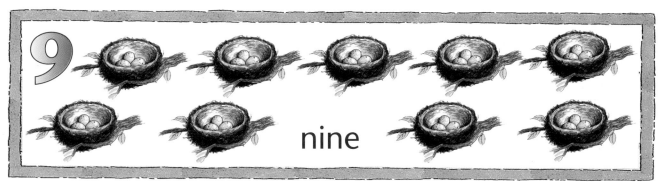
9 nine

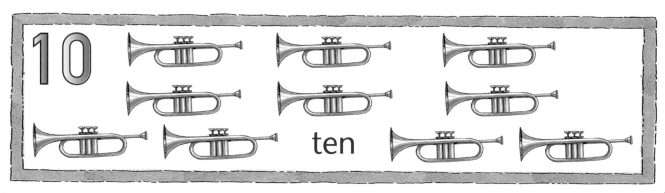
10 ten

## a
airport
ambulance
ant
apple
apron
arm

## b
baby
bag
ball
balloon
banana
basket
bath
beach
beans
bed
bee
bicycle
bird
black
blue
boat
book
boy
bread
bridge
brown
butter
butterfly
button

## c
calf
camel
castle
cat
caterpillar
chair
clown
computer
cow
crab
crayons
crocodile
cup

## d
desk
dice
dinosaur
dog
doll
dolphin
donkey
door
dragon
dress
drum
duck

## e
ear
egg
eight
elephant
envelope
eyes

## f
feather
fire
fish
five
flowers
fly
foal
foot
forest
fork
four
fox
frog
fruit

## g
garden
gate
ghost
girl
glass
globe
glove
gorilla
grass
grasshopper
green
guitar

## h
half
hamburger
hammer
hand
hat
head
helicopter
hen
hippopotamus
hole
horse
house

## i
ice cream
icicle
insects
iron
island

## j
jacket
jam
jeans
jeep
jigsaw
jug

## k
kangaroo
kettle
key
king
kite
kitten
koala

## l
ladder
lamp
leaf
lemon
lion
lizard

## m
magnet
man
map
mask
microwave
milk
mirror
monkey
monster
Moon
mountain
mouse
mushrooms

## n
nail
necklace
needle
nest
nine
nurse
nuts

## o
octopus
one
onion
orange
ostrich
owl

## p
paint
paper
parachute
pear

peas
pencil
penguin
piano
picture
pie
pillow
pineapple
pink
plant
puppet
puppy
purple

## q
quarter
queen
question mark
quilt

## r
rabbit
radio
rain
rainbow
red
ring
river
robot
rocket
ruler

## s
sandwich
saw
scissors
seven
six
skeleton
snail
snake
snowman
sock
spider
spoon
star
stool
string
submarine
sun
swing

## t
table
tadpole
tail
teddy bear
telephone
television
ten
three

tiger
tomato
toothbrush
towel
toys
tractor
train
tree
trumpet
turtle
two

## u
umbrella
underwear
unicorn
uniform

## v
vacuum cleaner
vase
vegetables
video
violin
volcano

## w
watch
water
waterfall
whale
wheel
wheelbarrow
white
windmill
window
woman
wood

## x
X-ray
xylophone

## y
yacht
yawn
yellow
yo-yo

## z
zebra
zero
zig-zag
zoo